MAKING MUSIC

Written by
Bernadette Parkhurst-Smith

THE SCIENCE OF PERCUSSION INSTRUMENTS

KidHaven
PUBLISHING

Published in 2027 by
KidHaven Publishing, an Imprint of Greenhaven Publishing, LLC
2544 Clinton St., Buffalo, NY 14224

Written by: Bernadette Parkhurst-Smith
Edited by: Rebecca Phillips-Bartlett
Designed by: Ker Ker Lee

Cataloging-in-Publication Data

Names: Parkhurst-Smith, Bernadette.
Title: The science of percussion instruments / Bernadette Parkhurst-Smith.
Description: Buffalo, NY : KidHaven Publishing, 2027. | Series: Making music | Includes glossary and index.
Identifiers: ISBN 9781534570283 (pbk.) | ISBN 9781534570290 (library bound) | ISBN 9781534570306 (ebook)
Subjects: LCSH: Percussion instruments--Juvenile literature.
Classification: LCC ML1030.P375 2027 | DDC 786.819--dc2

Printed in China

CPSIA compliance information: Batch #QS27KH: For further information contact Greenhaven Publishing LLC at 1-844-317-7404.

Please visit our website, www.greenhavenpublishing.com.
For a free color catalog of all our high-quality books, call toll free 1-844-317-7404 or fax 1-844-317-7405.

Find us on

Photo Credits – Images courtesy of Shutterstock.com, unless otherwise stated.

Cover & Recurring – RidiUmbrella, hatsak, Galih Yoga Wicaksono. 2–3 – Iryna Inshyna. 4–5 – Nataliia__photo, Gary J. Bush. 6–7 – Janeberry, PeopleImages.com - Yuri A. 8–9 – Daniel Jarosch, Kandybka Alina. 10–11 – Krakenimages.com, Manuel Milan. 12–13 – Panjarong Urawan, AlvaroRT. 14–15 – All Music Instruments, Petrychenko Anton. 16–17 – Good dreams - Studio, sarawuth wannasathit. 18–19 – amy.lezama, daseaford. 20–21 – Eza_Nanda, Dejan Dundjerski. 22–23 – Studio Light and Shade, Dizfoto.

CONTENTS

Words that look like this can be found in the glossary on page 24.

SOUND AND SCIENCE

How do musical instruments make such interesting sounds? What is the secret to making music? It turns out there is no secret to it. It can all be explained by science!

Let's find out what happens when we play musical instruments.

This book is all about percussion instruments. To play these instruments, you hit, shake, or scrape them. Many percussion instruments are used to make the beat that the music follows.

WHAT ARE SOUNDS?

A sound is a vibration. A vibration is when something moves back and forth very quickly. Just like a wave moves through water, vibrations can move through instruments and air. This is called a sound wave.

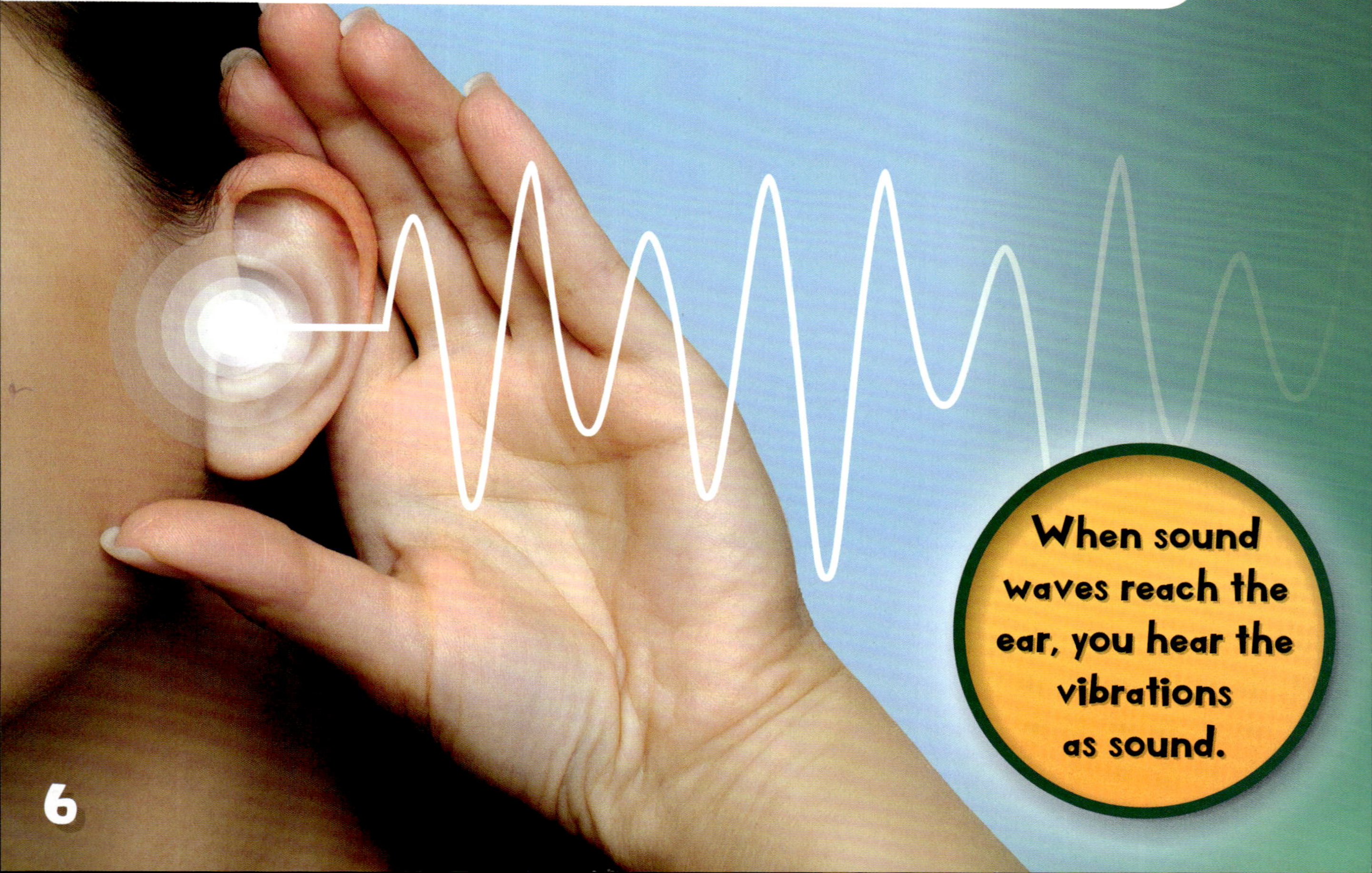

To play a percussion instrument, you shake it or hit it with your hands or a stick. This makes the instrument vibrate, which creates sound waves.

Hitting percussion instruments in a repeating pattern is how music gets its rhythm.

TAMBOURINE

A tambourine is a small type of drum. A drum is an instrument with a tightly stretched sheet across it. The sheet is called a head or skin. Today, a tambourine head is typically made from plastic.

A long time ago, tambourine heads were made from animal skin.

The metal discs are called jingles.

When you hit the head, it vibrates. This sends sound waves through the air. You can also shake the tambourine to make the metal discs bang together. This makes a ringing sound.

MARACA

A maraca is a type of percussion instrument called a rattle. You hold the handle and shake the maraca. Inside, tiny balls bounce off the sides, which creates the vibrations.

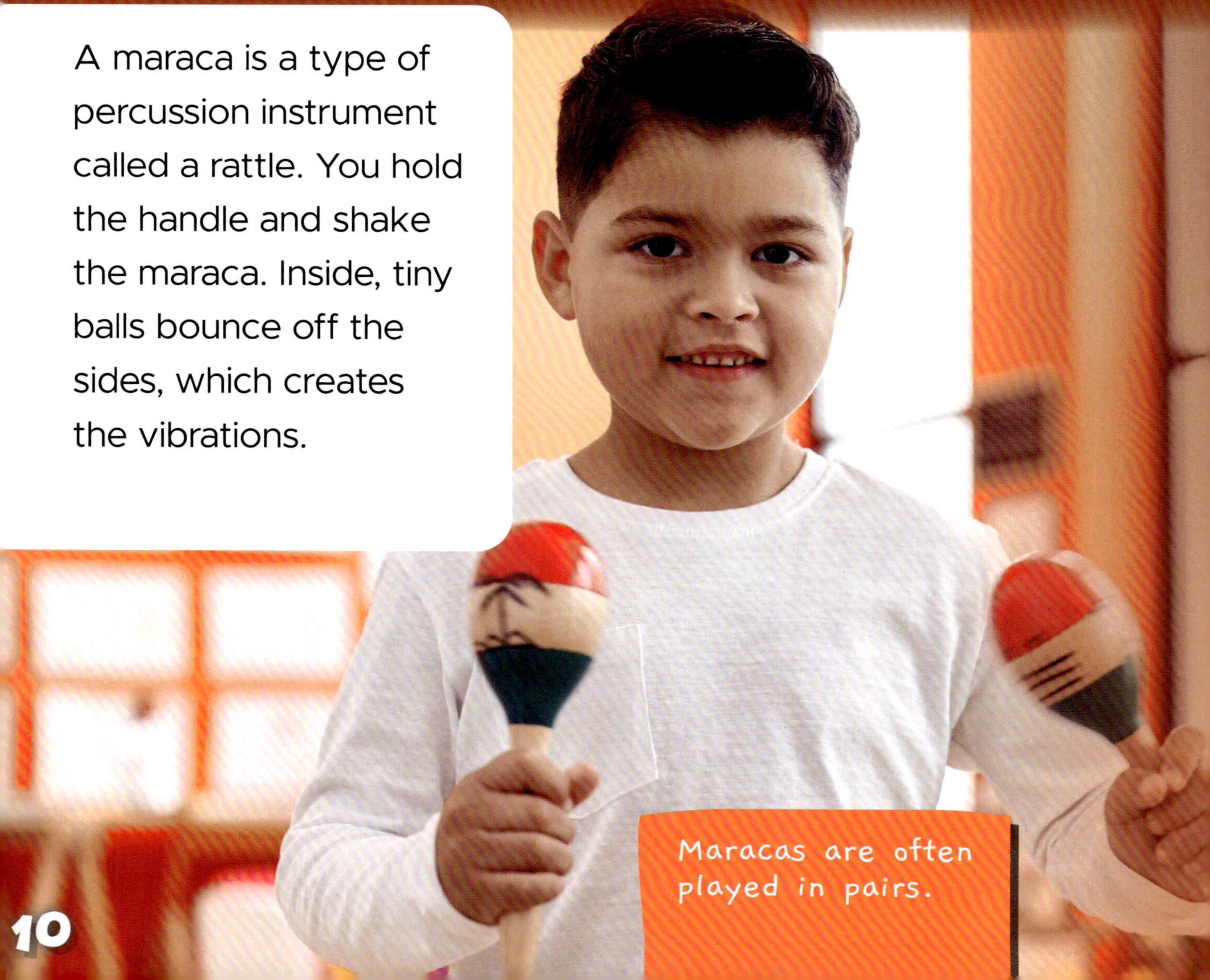

Maracas are often played in pairs.

If you shake the maracas harder, the balls inside will hit the sides with more force. This will create stronger vibrations, which means the sound will be louder.

Some maracas are made from gourds with seeds, beans, or stones inside.

CONGA

A conga is a long, narrow type of drum. It has a tightly stretched skin, or head, that you hit with your hands. The body of a conga is called the shell.

The shell is usually made of wood.

You make different sounds by hitting different areas of the head. The sound also changes based on whether you hit it with the palm of your hand or your fingers. The head vibrates, which vibrates the air inside the shell.

Some people can play up to three congas at a time.

MARIMBA

A marimba has a row of wooden bars called tone plates. You hit the tone plates with sticks with soft ends called mallets. The tone plates vibrate, which also vibrates the air around them.

Soft mallets help make a gentle sound.

A marimba makes musical notes. Each note has a different pitch. Shorter tone plates make quicker vibrations, creating higher-pitched notes. Longer tone plates make slower vibrations, which creates lower-pitched notes.

Underneath are resonator pipes, which make the notes louder.

GONG

A gong is a big metal circle. You play the gong by hitting it with a soft mallet. The vibrations start where the gong is hit. They spread to the edges, then into the air.

Gongs are often used in temples.

Many gongs are hung in the air using ropes or cords. This lets the metal vibrate freely. The sounds of a gong can last a long time because nothing stops the vibrations.

Some gongs can be very big.

STEELPAN

The steelpan is a metal percussion instrument. It can create musical notes that have different pitches. You play the steelpan by hitting the curved piece of metal with sticks.

Inside a steelpan, there are lots of dents. The dents have been carefully tuned by being hammered into different sizes and shapes. Each dent creates a note with a different pitch.

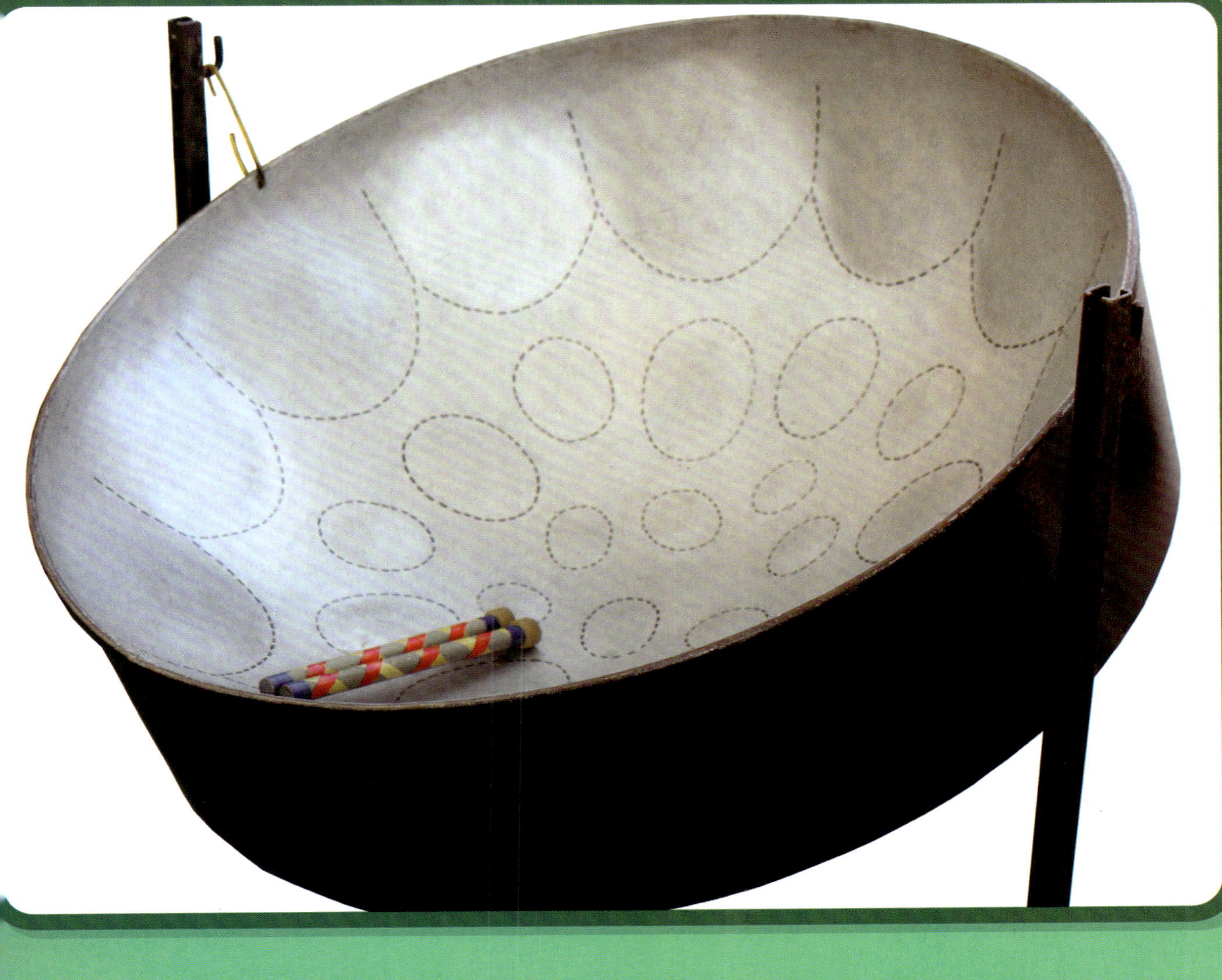

DRUM KIT

A drum kit is a collection of percussion instruments put together. You use sticks to hit the skin of the snare drum and tom-toms. You can also hit the metal cymbals.

The kick drum makes a big, deep sound. It is hit by a mallet when you press a pedal with your foot. Lots of genres of music use a drum kit.

SPOONS

Did you know spoons can be musical instruments? When holding two spoons, you can tap them with your hand or on your leg. This bangs them together, making them vibrate.

Some spoons are specially made for music. Normal spoons work too.

You have now learned a lot about how percussion instruments make sounds. It is time to make some of those sounds yourself. Choose your instrument, and start making music!

Lots of everyday objects can be instruments if you know how to play them!

GLOSSARY

beat a steady sound, usually made by percussion instruments, that acts as the pulse of music

force a push or pull on an object

genres styles or types of art

gourds big fruits that have hard skin

notes musical sounds with a high or low pitch

rhythm a pattern of sounds, usually made by percussion instruments, that follows the music's beat

temples places of worship

tuned when an instrument or object is changed to play musical notes with the right pitch

INDEX